Lotus Mandala & The Basorexia Song

Z.M. Wise

World Inkers Printing and Publishing
Senegal, Africa
New York, New York

Copyright © 2024, Z.M. Wise.

.

Contents of this publication remain the intellectual property of Z.M. Wise. None of these works may be reproduced in any format, whether electronically or in print, without consent from the publisher World Inkers Printing and Publishing or Z.M. Wise, except as portions in reviews.

Contact publisher's representative Dustin Pickering:
publication.worldinkers@gmail.com

Front and back cover art by Nancy Weiss

ISBN-13: 978-2-487017-07-8

Lotus Mandala & The Basorexia Song

Z.M. Wise

Other Works by Z.M. Wise

POETRY:

The Pleasant Dreamers

The Nightmare Mask

Illinois Infinitarium

Kosmish and the Horned Ones

Cuentos de Amor: 25 Observational Years of Experience in Continuity

Wolf: An Epic and Other Poems

The Wandering Poet

Take Me Back, Kingswood Clock!

ALBUM:

Ch'ulel(with A.J. Kaufmann)

PLAY:

Bottles of Emerald for the Demon Queen

The Falling Contents

Introduction: Juxtapoesy

I have always marveled at the idea of two polar opposites being united in some form or fashion, whether it was a hero and villain fighting on the same side or an unlikely romantic pairing. It is both amusing and thought-provoking. In this particular case, two longform pieces appear in the same volume of verse, the former being a confessional piece that was an expanded version of a poem within a notebook and the latter being a nonlinear epic (with song lyrics at the bittersweet end), also acting as the expanded version of another notebook poem. The concepts themselves could not be any more different. Two countries in total opposition hold each other's hands for but a brief series of fleeting moments. Who could ask for anything more? I maintain the opinion that the reverse magnetic effect that contradictory mindsets have on one another is a subconscious delight.

Without revealing a significant portion of detail, *Lotus Mandala* addresses the unconventional and all too real issue of limerence. In layman's terms, 'limerence' is infatuation amplified, an unhealthy obsession with someone. To the limerent person, they will perceive this as love, while the recipient of such toxic energy serves the unfortunate role of 'the limerent object'. Limerence is far from a diagnosable condition, per se, but it affects the mental health of numerous individuals. The character within the poem realizes he has struggled with this invisible parasite throughout most of his life. That being said, as he sheds these layers, he experiences the ultimate epiphany: he has found something higher than love for a partner, and that such a love is not what the populace has dreamed into existence. This love is none other than love of the self. No human on Earth can enhance or complement it. It is the ultimate revelation, the silent answer he has craved for what seemed like millennia. In the romantic sense, it is liberation from traditional and societal standards.

The Basorexia Song, on the other hand, is optimistic hypocrisy, seen through the lens of an ironical monocle. However, I have one question for you, Dearest Reader: when you find yourself locked in a dream that plays out as a surreal odyssey between you and your partner, does your honorary degree in lucid dreaming aid you in the process of controlling said dream, or does *it* control *you*? Enough said. *Paxvobiscum.*

Z.M. Wise

Lotus Mandala: Forgetting Limerance Layers

"If you treat the overarching psychological root causes of limerence, on the other hand, you are guaranteed to leave the condition behind and surface as a new, more resilient, cheerful version of yourself."
- Anonymous Psychologist

"Those without personal knowledge of limerence explained the strange actions of limerents as the results of romantic, imaginative, fantasy. They called it storybook-like, unreal, romantic, the product of artistic imagination, poetic hyperbole, or vagueness. Sometimes the writing better fit the non-limerent perspective, sometimes they described limerence. It is not hard to see why a taboo has surrounded the study and analysis of love. No one feels entirely comfortable with the subject, both limerents and non-limerents among my interviewees suspected there was something going on they didn't know about, something they took as a personal failing. The limerent interpreted non-limerent external behaviour as self-composure. Self-confidence, individuality, independence, and mind over irrational desire. The non-limerent was not viewed as a person who does not desire, but as one whose moral fiber does not allow passion to rule over reason. When non-limerents told limerents to stop being silly and forget a love interest who is not worth it, and not interested – the limerents tried to obey. They couldn't; but couldn't believe that they couldn't."
- Dorothy Tennov

Love,
that court jester's tumbling
head sailing 'cross Orion's
belted borders while the
Sisters Kristal and Crystal
cry Mother Mountain Superior
hymns on faded stages.
This storm has only begun.

It has begun in the colosseum of universal
brinks, tipping point, my
sweet neck kiss of subconscious
rage, moaning claw marks on
my courtship back, only half
a beast of burdened deprivation.

Can we forgive the past
for splitting ganglion heads
and shattering multiverses of my war?

You wanted my cold and calculated heart.
You wanted my Sumerian insignia.

Universal neurosis monger
reaching involuntary apotheosis,
enlightenment self-expansion.

Disenchantment, love's banality.
Horizons broadening over her
Gaia shoulder, the lips of ambiguous truth.
Mi Corazon, tu dulzura es mi calavera.

O' the Hounds of Heaven and
the *paradiso* of earthly hell,
sway the splendor'd arches,
bathing in the Aging Fountain,
youth abandoned on June 24,
matricide in mass hypnosis.

Down the nocturnal name
and up the diurnal daylight.

Prehistory gliding through the air
on reptilian backs and
avian wingspan faith,
faith in the betrayal of myself.

Unlearned teachings in *amor*,
help me to help myself.
Cynical cyanide and jaded jadestone,
give me to the Nether,
bring me to the Never.

To shed eighty-eight skins
and be rebirthed as a crescent
Selene echoing the dance of laughter.

Starlight lords bowing before
celestial ladies who will
never incinerate themselves,
like Helios, solar sphere of us all.

Everything is finite on this
astral tether, anxious attachment
to a realm of transparency.
Let physicality ride itself
until climax claims its hold
on partnership superficiality,
societal reject of love.

Eight metals of fleeting minds,
one for each banshee O scream.

Visitations of dripping silver,
heated candlewax on fruitful
bounties of ocular bedroom shock.

The favored nudity, the
exalted montage
of post-coital hushed whispers
so the Ophanim cannot hear.
Be not afraid?

Fear the sacred geomantic shield,
hindering advancement and
seeking the womb of the cocoon.

No metamorphosis but the
titanic blossoming of desolate
headspace, sandstorm of
livid lava, magma's morality.

Singing chasm death songs,
death in this fortress'd hole.

Orifice of oracular indecision,
I am only as trusting as my void,
ever-altering sexual chameleon,
situational haunter thrashing
about in symphonic doom,
slashing about in the slopes
of progressive black death.

Melodies scattering about
like fragmented wolves,
belting out labyrinthine cries
save Theseus rope for *Canis* noose.

So, hear this orison and despair:
"Love's rose petals of toxicity,
shower your gifts and presence
upon those who hunger for you."

Hunger for you, once did I,
in pathetic Cupid commands,
at every turn, at every
sigh of concrete angelic acknowledgment.

How could I bear to
reveal this rabid face,
rabid for the stone tablets of
your shadow figurehead?
Bravado exceeded, the spilling
of ink words, be damned.

Ink words, be damned.
Ink words, be quick.
Ink words immortalized
like onion layers of limerence laid on thick.

Stain glass religion shattering
windows of rosy petals.

Trek on Atlantean current.
Venture a highway.
Pale passageways of Artemis,
the crimson wound of Jupiter.

Gateways burning with artificial gold,
to part the ways of
dancing sanctuary and dulcet chatter.

Once shelter in your arms,
now tangled barbwire vines,
the wrath of grapes, rumored fermentation.

Dialogues with the dawn in
the asylum of your sacred kiss.
Lips of salvation, heal my
orison glass sprinting 'cross my wrists.

The Lover of Tremendous Value,
you people and your fickle sickle.
You trust mongers, instilling fear
in the counted tree trunk rings
of my saturated sanity.

Sanity is a ghost of lusting death.
Loyalty's deceit in the
cavity of innermost wilderness.

Lady Lover, drift with me,
drift with me,
as we bask in the
savannahs of the sea.
Lady Lover, converse with me,
about the demolishment of the patriarchy.
Lady Lover, salvage me,
from the judge's finger of societal purity.
This is just a matrushka dream,
concept upon concept until
the Oneness binds itself to thee.

Flee me down, Tremendous Paramour.
Flee me down, Dubious Metamour,
until the Archer misses
us and envelops the
bystander of Druidian trees,
lifting vulnerability veils
and slashing them in two.

Driven by hoofbeat thunder
in the plains where I seek
solitary refuge, sexual solace
in the warmth of your
thousand-eyed embrace.
"You have always occupied my head,"
the metallic-winged angel hath spake.

Every love song, dedicated to
the upward prism of myself.
Every love story's conclusion,
holding myself close my soul,
overthrowing the sanctified throne,
usurping the majestic faces
commandeering this meat vessel.

Look! My faces are one!
They have melded, flaming luck!
Voice about the melodious
synchronicity of motionless chrome.

In the face of jovial madness,
I came to be a
sacrificial sperm feast.

Promise my silhouette
to the dusk and unfurl
for the fellowship of sweet caresses.

Ecstatic skin speaking
in sentimental *serpentes* tongues.

Pluck my seraphim feathers
from my hyperphantasia clouds,
nine falling on burning beds,
lips acquainting one another.

Chalices of unholiness reeking
of romantic intentions as
sipped from the mouths of babes,
babes in the forbidden woods
where my failed innocence
committed the justifiable homicide
it needed, o' how we moved forward.
Plunging 'neath the depths
where the apex king of my
scalding heart thirsts for
another mortal detriment.

Azure paling in comparison
to the magenta sky of
dystopian utopia,
no conflict with death's
cinnabar banquet, weeping for consumption.

Become one with me,
invisible doppelganger clinging
to the shell of a decomposing of self,
arise from the detritus of
millennia of wall writing,
unanswered, platonic questions,
verbose vernacular in mathematical
jargon, the light from oral bards
and silent orators of speaking pictures.

Sky ground rotating the
four seas, for I have been
lost in yours, the suffering
of your mutated gaze,
Dickensian poverty per page,
Spenserian queenie ruling
o'er a country of none.

Write me off in rabid
stanzas of abrupt foam,
oceans ending, intervening
with the idol of false divinity.

You have seen the color of my voice
as jaded pewter, carved with
our amalgamation of monikers.

Your face was the poem I
could not read whilst
doggy paddling through the layered voids.

Be my lapsed maven in
the darkest arts, O'
Parter of Grandest Canyons.

I am the other side of
the ghost hand who caresses
your cheek of apocalyptic scars,
the transparent lips who
relieve the aspiration of
meeting yours in psychic gratification.

This night's moonlight millennium
will never be witnessed again.

Hungry ghosts of starvation,
harpy hellspawn in majik.

This death sentence is for
too prolonged, running on
fumes spewed from the
stoned mouths of ganja gorgons.

Never let go in the city
you dream of, mirrored and
lingering in the star-crossed,
silken spread-eagle duality.

It's a monster, insatiable
to the superficial desires it craves.
It's a monster, but only
to the dark skies it created
out of psychosis sessions.
It's a monster, for
it was me in a human suit.

Accursed shell in dire
need of birth cracking,
rebirthed and redeathed,
in reverse ouroboros cycle.
Mandarin characters in mid-century,
puncturing galactic flight boundaries
with star liner harmony.

But, I was never in my head
to begin with, for the
dais of luminescent ramblings
takes hold of me,
the tidal arms of Neptune,
a wilting rose sinking down
to a pressurized grave of implosion.

The delusions of dusk began
at dawn's moaning bell,
climactic chimes for
necropolitan thinking, O'
Head of Prominent Precision.

Tomorrow's promise cherubs,
quadrupeds and sanctifying
the glimmering dead's words of dust.

Laughing in the eyes of grief,
Goddess's Cosmos and I wept simultaneously.
A tearful purge for the art
of blinding voyeuristic spectators.

Fostering the Faustian for
Mephistophelean method,
upfront gifts in Satanic blessings.
She was always a judge
of none appearing before
the resurrection of tragedy.

Flaming arrows of Hell on Earth.
We have made one for ourselves,
a bird's eye collective view
of mortal individualization.
Naiveté of the Goddess Transition.

Hear my Rubik's Cube plea
and morph my fauna moth
into floral gestures that
show themselves before worth,
suitors of petal plucking,
sprites in burlesque faerie space.

Ah! But stirring sound in
exemplary existence charging
like the *toro* to the unclothed,
bosomed shroud of the air,
the comfort of flesh warmth
drowning in *idiomas de amor*.

Sky watchers in the tendencies
of her sighing body in
their climactic pinnacle
I will never be acquainted with.

The blissful milk of
human kindness *in absentia*,
delicate speed, the foal of
totem inconsistency.

A voice's psychedelic waves come to thee,
for the owner is the inner me.

I am self-love after dark,
fornicating the sky, yet
smitten with the sea.

Haunted by terrestrial gasps,
rune readers in ruination.

A smile colored blind,
taking caravan rides 'cross
peyote desert land with
an uncharted *paradiso* of teal.

To read the book of faces
is to succumb to virtual hell.

Be my digital iconoclast.
Be my keyboard warrior assassin.
Let words of arrows soar
like orphan dragons toward
an angelic virginal cave
whose treasure was shallow venom.

Will she ring the Pavlovian
bells of the conditional cathedral?
Will she activate my
green valley routine sequences?
Will the anachronistic moonlight
awaken the lone wolf wonder
to greet the nude night with
moonrise heart throbbing
dentine deprivation in the depths.

Nothing can slake the
desert of lust's first gasp
but the goddess's silken corpse.
Nothing moves me like
the descent of her curves
unperturbed stillness in the face.

Statue of the flesh
nary a societal flaw,
but she is no more than
a shadow game in quickened
majestic insistency…
The cloud's magical jest
bringing me to my faltering knees,
smitten with the discovered self
and only him.

Defenseless 'gainst musical trust.
Youth is but a means to
a beginner's fantasy in the
snowblind sacrifice of reality.

Death of the lute and lyre,
the shorn lamb's newbown,
the torn ram's skull horn.
Love lies bleeding in
the jesting lamb we have shorn,
the protesting ram we have scorned,
for the horn we blow is
Amaranthine hill holiday melodies,
yielding to the wisest of swine,
the Entelodonts of intelligence.

Symbol of the Inventive Age,
am I the raconteur of
wavering smoke letter rings?

Stagnating mists of time
have come to rally around me.
The compass of sedentary direction,
the Infinite Designer and
jilted heart, left at a goddess's altar.

Suffer me no beauty but
the floral intoxication of her fingers.
Suffer me no sensation but
the bitter fruit of the tasteful, magnetic skin,
for I am into the pathos
of your chaos trumpet fanfare.

The pillaring voyage 'cross
the hammered eighth sea.
Destiny's children await
her final command, a
music-laden kamikaze farewell.

Molting myself, the only
cicada resurrection, the
rez of erection, risen like
monoliths of vanity in the
purest of stolen landscapes.

Rotting death and robust harvests,
brutal pursuit comes the hand
of ever-flowing flickers of glory,
now charred from my mouth word remains.

Beautiful, frowning thing,
gorgeous, futile thing,
the mirror world that separates
your reality from my golden apples of denial.

Let the sour damage the
sweet in a cataclysmic
blowout of world-ending Os.

Feral love needs human touch.
Human touch needs jovial screams.
Jovial screams need Aya purging.

Cognitive mother, omnipresent
in all courageous carnage.

Dearest Implosion of the Night,
reflexes in reflection
of electric current confession papers.

Salvage me and only me!
Leave the previous self for
June embers of annual birth.
The *naga* voice of her sex,
consuming me whole for
the self-destruction of arthouse theatre.

To fancy her would be
fateful suicide songs,
playing out of masterful tune
and into vacated astral specimens.

The clasping of her shaded gloves,
turning a hue of speed white,
fond of your definitive outline,
blinded by toxic positivity.

Weakened for sabotaged arousal.
Footfall off every dream cliff
extending to the vacillated
that we face, evolution
waning like bashful moons
sans thirteen reasons to conform.

The Fathers of Lies removed
the invisible smile from the
sphere upon that which we stand.
Instincts succumbing to
systemic injustices that
their hands, rank and scarred,
commit with no effort,
O’ my oblivious children bones.

Wisest of the peacemakers
waging war on the self
‘fore we are praising evil waters
for their rejuvenating purity.
Drink you into seven dimensions later.

Let this bountiful judgment
through *el cancion de la Reina*,
ruling *mi Corazon* as it were.

I see nothing but battles
in kaleidoscopic, arthropod eyes,
a more savage loveline cut
off on amputated shrieking hands.

Tell us why we see not
through a candelabra fire's
pure elegance, the luminosity
of a universal maddening cry.

To weep is to celebrate humanity's blessed curse.
The loneliness of crowded company.
To shut you all out, an authentic pleasure
of the Liberated Bronze Age.

Flashback to a mechanical future
with organic, carnal ambitions.

The regal parasite is no more!
The layered love, peeled back,
reveals the oneness of solitudinarian euphoria.

May 8-May 25, 2024

The Basorexia Song: A Nonlinear Epic

“*And you see a girl’s brown body,*
dancing through the turquoise,
and her footprints make you follow
where the sky loves the sea.
And when your fingers find her,
she drowns you in her body,
carving deep blue ripples
in the tissues of your mind.”
- Cream

Basorexia: Initium Novum (New Beginning)

Lady *Verde*,
midday gown kneeling past
this poem's stone sky evening.

With great hesitation comes
greater confessional beginnings.

You would be the Artemis
I wake up to past devilish clock,
sacrilegious geometry shapes are hands,
the hips you sway against me
during silent speech dances.

This reality, as surfaced as golden strands
sliding down your summer hills.

To ride the earliest train
a-swifting, your weary head
on my dimensional chest as
the gift of insanity unwraps itself.

Soul bond to the water birth,
infantile maturation, we have
surpassed the shoulder's ice plateau.

O' Basorexia, presence absorbing
future treasure marks
like some faulty wizard,
transfixed by the majik of your laughing sigh.

August 8, 2024

I

This hushtone kiss falls
over the deafest clairaudient's
ears of generational wisdom.

There she walks,
my beautiful life,
torn asunder to discover
passive illumination at
the end of time's ebon tunnel.

Tragedy falters to strike,
though the fiery embrace of
her amorous arms send
me spinning in vertigo virility.

If you could absorb my
vacated conch shell echo,
would the ocean's torrential voice
guide you to the plains of
our field rebirth,
the merriment of meadows
frolicking in anti-summer breezes?
We are the lullaby of tomorrow's forever.

To be thalassophiles together,
devotees of the existential sea,
cosmic Helios eye staring unto thee.

I think in green,
but the blue of Poseidon
washes over my mind like
a tidal summer scene.

You are an unmasked guise,
Woman Dreamscape Lips,
an unlit torch to ignite the
beacons of neophyte love.

Remove your glove of the past
and raise truth's sword,
reforged from the gullet sky.

I have kissed the air for
more years than sand stars.
I have made love to shadows
more nights than golden jaguar heads.

Solitudinarian serenity,
the 9.8 tremor of instrumental perfection.

Raging over Aztec fire,
your original name spilling out
from Quetzalcoatl's essence.

Quetzalcoatl, the
Mother of you all under
the solar rays where we met,
for our parallel hands shook
in gothic birthday mystery,
clad in midnight draped o'er
my polychromatic feathered heart.

Bloodstream Queen,
Reina de la Sangre,
oozing out suneye pyramid children.

The time we shed is
the silverback oilskin.
The silverback oilskin
that slide off our Mediterranean flesh
is an undertow, waiting
to devour us in toothless heaven.
Dressed like a *bruja* seer,
conjurer of petaled roots,
the striped acrobat of loving gazes.

Gorgeous as life, but
a warlord of every tampered death.

Trust in me, thrust in you,
and our mind's amalgamate
into regal sentience.

Stalking the slithering sane,
chariot feet carrying us faster
than privileged fire on land of the Original Exemplars.

Winged, hermetic feet flying
us to alternative mortality.
Congregation of sea wolves
to rally together, celebratory howl,
for we have reached the
pinnacle of momentary nirvana.

Your claws of ice, sating
my volcanic malnourishment.
I cannot see past your nightshade turn.

Tell me I am the memory of us,
being absorbed by the only
weaver of words, now a lone
vagabond running 'gainst a typhoon.

Earthen daughters' limbs,
hanging in the balance of
giving trees and reciprocal rivers
on your hopeless romantic chest,
leaves of elm and elder wood,
the wisdom of oak and succulence of maple,
licked clean with a gasp
of darkest mythology.
Storms of silk raining down
satin metamorphoses,
tangled in Arachne's webbed world.

A box of honey,
flowing in sustenance.

How we bathe in Mephistophelean bargains,
Circles Nine and Princes Four,
Harpies Three and Temples Two, and I am an
inverted universalist preaching
the word of individualized truths.

Stallion of Vatican wood,
guarding the forbidden textual nothing.

Jest me in the sanctum of
captured perfectness where their hope
will swallow us whole like
a planetary relinquishment.

I forgot about your tablet-read hand,
you metal messiah, you snowfall temptress,
you finger cymbal, you tingsha courtesan.

I will be your seven-headed
whore for the prosperity of Babylon.
I will be your waltzing battle
sword on the misty highways of Avalon.

We rally together for the gypsy travelers
who show us fortuitous pioneers' wanderlust
in crystal carvings and
T'ang Dynasty scribblings.

O' let us fly perilously with
the necromancers of old,
breathing the death of life
into the lifeless bones of war.
Melting steel into fluid love,
reading stoneground runes for
divination dancers, tampering
with realms that are not yet theirs.

Sculptured doom is not our
synthetic fate, but an
Amontillado wall of tombs,
sealing us in our final room,
back to the time of the astral womb.

Gushing springs at the free,
grasp of a lover's will.

Sabotage my riding logic
for a night song composed
on a Jane Doe tongue of brief remembrance.

The craving of You is not yet known,
your blinding breasts of luminescence,
softest light caresses after
nature's clock stops halfway.

Halcyonic dreams forming
in my mouth's last dark horse word,
This is what the mages breathe.

Catacombs hewn in skull throne
fashion sense, and we are the
center of all night air riding.

Ruffled our feathers and
we rise gently as phoenix lovers
in the glistening winter inferno.
Stood by ablaze in a violet daze.

This is what the prophets said.
This is what the prophet's head
uttered under severed thought.
Eyes of a warzone metal,
staring a thousand yards away
into amorous trauma fields,
the half-hearted limbs
aching for a rogue high affair,
pining for the needles of still lust.

We are all that remains
in the summer doll delight.

Take my moonshot hand,
climb out of my psyche's cavity,
and sing the hymns of contemplation.
Dance the *bachata* of stagnation.

Your cobra-lined eyes align
with the gatekeepers of fate.

Let our Mother, the Sky,
decide our place betwixt
the moss gardens and
the dampened earthen quietude.

Lady Archer misses thrice,
the insomniac arrows
thrashing about and
piercing love's neglected followers.

Spell Breaker,
your incantations merely rhyme.
Time Maker,
your finite hands nearly cliché.
Spirit Taker,
victimizing your own mirrored self.

You have known of such devilry,
the angelic masks as
fragrant as limerence itself.

Pungent Princess of Cross-Eyed Lies…
Away! Away! We bid thee adieu.

To the desert monoliths
that stand proud like the
omega outcasts in a village
of farcical familiarity

To the undersea obelisk
that remains statuesque
guardian for Atlantean conspiracies.

To the glass of *vino rojo*
with which we symbolize
our collective texture,
the translation of our
fingertip faces forming the
door we longed for…

The façade of fun,
the shroud of gasping mortality.

A newfangled town of facets
is ours for the giving,
for we are an astral fusion machine.

Bodies in the twilight of stone,
grasping for the concluding breath
of fading flesh in green noise.

Magenta silk, enveloped in
crimson satin, encased by the night.
Sandalwood brown combing
the desert flora for
one drop of oasis authenticity.

The quintessential dew kismet,
the archetypal horned Kosmish,
windows and forest kings,
wolves and pleasant dreamers.

Sweetest tongue uttering
words from a bitter language.
The elixir of dialect, flotation
from interpreter to receiver,
blistering suns setting on
a pariah horizon, ready
to broaden with might beyond red.

Become the bloodshed night,
for I am your hapless devotee.
Hell on Earth needs us,
for a surface-level chasm
is where we slumber
with lonely eyes no more.

There but for the majesty
of climactic passion, go I.

Consider the blessed curse
of dawn's nation rally,
smitten by your easing storm
as your eyes of melting
sweetness rest 'gainst my synthetic
puzzle piece diminishment.

Unarticulated syllables
escape not from my
lapsed judgment lips.

Can we levitate in the
American atmosphere,
soiling no more the sacred ground
that lost its potency and purity
when alabaster pierce
a once impenetrable force?
Can we remove the
art of unlimited discrimination,
the science of legendary segregation?

Can we hold each other's
hypocritical hands and
call this a proud united land?

Can we call our unity
'love in the time of
paradoxical elation'?

Do we deserve not the
approval of Venus's tall grass
of eyelashes, tickling our
fancy and brushing our
cheeks with the scents
of free will and majik?

The treasonous season spreads
sinister wings like
a Kipling vulture, ready
to scavenge on the
eagle's prayer feathered flesh,
for forfeiting to a higher avian power.

They separated from
toxicity's state of mind.

Lament for the lips we
tasted on spring berry mornings.
Santa Muerte, be praised
and humbled with humanist love.
Her rain songs and modesty dances
sweep one *cumbia* number
off their Wendigo feet
of eternal burning blazes.

Ashes to ashes,
poems to songs,
Guru Lady bangs her wordless gong.

Dueling silhouettes for the
audience of scintillating shadows.

I've had it with the
disillusionment of modernity,
asphalt jungles and concrete
trails defying nature,
only to lead me directly to you,
the game of dazzlers for
which no prayer emerges victorious.

Metropolitan misfortunes, no more,
a gatehouse of wilderness,
remaining nameless for
the storied lives of us.

I am your perpetual mime,
screaming jubilant obscenities
with frenzied hands in
the art of silent sounds.

Marrow of my bones that
chilled with eagerness when
laying my head on your
Venus chest mountains,
reassurance and the warmth
of a home I daren't deserve.

Cherished for your undying
radiance left behind for
nary a second, *querida*.

Oh, jingo, I nearly lost
full sight of your picturesque
nobility, to guide me through
arroyos many with autonomous
sensory meridian response words
that I call my own.

Nightmare honey, between
your budding eyes that
bloom to blossom,
wilt to tilt a world of
profundity our way.

Catching gales in our
palm's loveliness for fear
of letting loose a cyclone
of heavenly consequences
and hellish rewards.

A word of blasphemy, we seek
to send to the forked ink tongues
of bardic infidels.

Knoweth thyself and be dust.
Knoweth thyself and be debris.

The white-stained bedchambers
leak the calming residue of virility,
breathing little death into
protruding outward, like life,
a mantis queen giving head[s]
to the soil below her domain.

Sing to me your demise of song,
your futility of the rave.

We would be Cosmos nothingness
if not for our magnetic
union of conjoined souls
without orison or hushed
universal manifestation.

Did I manifest our
triosphere guardians who
bear witness to our gazebo
slow dancing ritual, our
courtyard hyena echoes?

Did I manifest the profusion
of blackened pages that
narrate your material world
citizen portrayal?

Like a herd of wildebeest,
always a lobotomized motion
roaming where the swine may be.
Never the virtuous follower,
never the valiant warrior.

I gasp audible air as
your declaration lips settle
their roots on my desolate neck,
an arid badland of near-virginal
bursts of daylight where
zealous acolytes will forever be faithless.

II

This faithless kiss
has escaped many a pair
of trusting lips,
their secrets met with anguish.
Kiss of the fatalist,
the wary anti-natalist.

Your caramel breasts swaying
'gainst my maroon statue face,
the brown of your gripping hand
scratching the ivory of my back,
the universal language of choral vocalization,
mutual ego-shattering wetness of splendor.

From 9 to sky,
the eight worlds collide
to sensational impact,
reverse Pangaea on the
turning away of the lam.

Our obituary comes to life
in a reanimated effort,
gray-green glow staring
from the wishful guru eyes,
lost in an ornate miasma.

I hear your lights flickering,
King Autumn, for my
ocular soul windows blacken
from the flaming skies,
ignited by wooden women
in their most vibrant hour.

Heated love and subzero hate,
we held hands in a Jalisco reservoir,
a Veracruz river bed
as aesthetic contrast
consumed the dark of
metropolitan country breeze.

The adobo spice of your
fountain pen rain words
spills from your cumin and thyme tongues,
echoing the pastures of your
eclectic ancestry, the majik
cat sat singing fence post litanies.

El Gato Negro asks,
"*Es tu cabeza la Estrella*?"

Almost touched the shadow games
of the earth's underground chapter.

Mammoth enormity of your
soothsaying reply, lingering all
the decaying decades this week.

Prophets deeming logic to their
days, the Chicago Ten,
cyclone after cyclone, the
spiraling minions barreling towards
the tranquility of emerald skies.

Lamenting the dusk for
its stubborn routine darkness.
Sun-bleached skull of a rat,
transcribing hollow thoughts on
hallowed soil for the nature
of it all, for we are only
pawns, *mi Corazon*, pawns
to a predestined ending.

Nothing will bind us together
but the mere syllables of action.

Rabid foaming at the severed
mouth that a god comes full poem.
I invite you to break the law.

Lover of the first awareness,
second sight, third eye blinded
by mechanical orgasms.
I invite you to break the law,
for the ironclad bond we share
holds no place in my right cognizance
but the tantric sanctum.

Sanctuary screaming out
wordlings in a tongue that
belongs not to dentine denizens,
Gaia and her Green Men of
lush dryad promise pave way
for our forestrian bridge,
crossed without nary a
psychedelic charm calling.

Even in the dulcet dreams
of your melodic torch light gaze,
the world is my mind
and I was birthed into the
inverted conformist's paradise.

El Sonidito de los lobos
carving our union's moniker by
Lycan love incantations.

Tibetan tea orators sipping
the leaves of serenity in
favor of us, but the chaos
winds alter fortune into a
disastrous wielding Gaelic weaponry.

We are Western sheep begging
for Eastern spells, begging
to hear the common man's fanfare.

Indian dawns falling on Spanish dusks,
cobra mothers mating with jaguar fathers
in writhing temple pillars,
laboring for liquid chrome chapters.

Enamored with the manatees of humanity,
I met with witless minds
on the endymion value…
Socratic starstruck method,
Platonic galaxy friend,
now a partnership of seasonal
dreams in waking where
realities know not where
the 'upslide down' lies,
nor the labyrinthine ladders,
climbing down corners of
lips in centuries-old barrios.

They are of the forgotten tongue,
Toltec sacrifice on Lower Wacker,
Chicago's Sears Tower of Babel,
Shamans of the Atrio,
enlisting Western guidance
on the elevated luxury
within a dormant desire.

Tangled vine tavern
inviting us in for ancient
oases reveries, for at night,
the Bandit at the Embassy
relives nostalgic suspension
in sanctuary nightlight rumbles.

We smell like home, thank Goddess.
We smell of home, Cosmos Goddess preserve us.
We have surpassed balcony evergreens.
We have attained deity's view,
for rooftop celebration screams
decipher themselves in elation.

Metaphors of the stoneguard deep,
flatland plains never ours, perhaps
Midwest infinitarium opening,
its colosseum gates to let loose.

The Grecian urn odes, torn to pieces
by vomitarium tigers in the
breath of sacred safe spaces.
She cannot touch me until Hour Eight.

Sun arise, we know it all.
The nocturnal flight through
cloud curtains, demystifying
no greater philosophy than
the theory of us, limerent parasites be damned.

I shall tell you my only
Midwest Side Story with
an East Side seaside sound,
whisked away by the ravine.

Damaged goods decaying with
the best of us mystic bed brothers,
in the suburbs of my solitary whoredom,
I am a façade of alleyway faces.

Elated for Babylon's insanity,
we reshape our own shared ending,
regression for a medieval mess.

Illegal adventure for fame,
incognito train ride to the
ocean wave avenues.

Scratch my back of desire,
digging your feathered talons
into the spine cage where
I contemplate courage and
an unfettered yearning from
which there is no escape.

No survival, the midnight salt,
I taste your grains on
a hill of sugar, a light of lime.

Dance of the Sanguine Strigois,
fortress of fruitful *sangre*.
Peacemaking sage into
a heavenly cage of fueled rage.

So, this is the vault of escapism,
the fictitious truth that
turns every lie of love into
geographic realities.

Seminal friction 'gainst your
honey butter jar with an
ecstatic gasp of reassurance.

We are the chosen and forgotten,
putrid demon lovers in an
angelic field of sheeple miscreants.

Vicious circle rounded everything
out of snapping, flashing focus.

To be born a sheltered redbreast
with no salvation from above,
hermeticized with sealed secrets,
with orchard eyes and tanned Nazca lines,
solving a maze fortune line.

We rude one another into clandestine Saturday,
one blink of the midnight black,
sucking thumbs of the satyr,
the wind in my ingrained seed.

For when the looming wolves
entrance us with their grand entrance,
their sea legs, webbed and wandering,
fly through panther skies,
the musky scent of your inner thighs.
We groove like convulsing, embalmed corpses.

Pulsate like electric killers
in lightning chairs, for
pain has always screamed in harmony
with Bloodthorn Roses.

Ghostly Illini blessed my forehead
with OM, Orgasmic Meditation,
with dancing 'round fiery rain.

You sing to us of your beloved
Tzotzil Madre speech, pillaged and rubbed out.
From societal existence until
its heart of a wine bottle sunrise
burnt like a flickering bulb.

Not of this crooked world,
Dionysian dizziness visions, the
glowing teeth of the hedonist
descend into fallen state of grace.

Tethered to one another as
we erase moonlit stories from
cosmic requiems, tattered space age,
Abyssinia in sudden totality.

Earth eaters arising from
the crevasse where slumber
knows no astral boundaries.
And all I feel is the Inner You.

Suburbia songs echoing privilege poems
in light polluted street men,
claiming ownership of collective consciences.
And all I gasp for is the Inner You.

Black water symphonies playing
melodies of supernova geneses
in sketches of trumpeters' flamenco.
And all I desire is the Inner You.

Inner you of lust's infinite library,
teller of oral tomes 'gainst
my listening *serpentes* tongue.

Unburdening the vacant lot of
us for the commenced ascent,
a dimension of pleasure screams,
fingernails trailing down
your neophyte spines until
our self-portrait turns
horizontal for the landscape effect,
glistening scenery, a tattoo in
living color seeking permanence.

I am your poet and yours to
write off, splitting love into
non-hierarchal fourths on
witching hour sky-scented parchment.

Every day you have the
same meadow-romping dream of me,
spilling mutual starseeds on
dewdrop dawn grounds.

No greater whisper
than the choir of your name.
No gentler breeze
I could wish for more
than the gust of your hands.

Nuclear war in the
forefront of your dark realm,
nestling against my cheek of longing.

Impetus of our synergy,
the connectivity of exuberance,
the bond of our aging word.

Sweltering heat of our existence
rises like Helios on the
cusp of climate's final change.

Mutual choreography cleans
the feet of proper soil,
flaunting the generational hand claps.

And now we float down
the Tiger River as Japanese paper memories,
the sprits of poesy unwritten.

Downpour of melodies in
a musical deluge lost
in my head of incongruity.

Cloudbursting euphoric death choices.
All as merciless as the
destroyer Shiva and believers
of the harvester Kali.
Who will you dream yourself into tonight?

Curse my battleground
for the sake of blessed specters.
Remove me limb from limb
as a selfless giving tree.

Take our harvest apples
for succulent sustenance,
our branches for shielding shelter,
our leaves for Green Man gasps.

With humbling reverence,
we kiss each other away
into unmentioned dimensions.

Theory in thievery: your first words
robbed me of a stampeding organ,
vitals in utter submission,
yet dominated by fire books
outgunned by the sea
of public piranhas in an outrage nation.

The future of grief
lies at a loss of hellish balance,
a tumbling standstill.

Meditations on the lake of oneness,
lambs feasting on lions
for evolutionary progressions.

Dragonnas goddess and bird maiden ask,
“How do you know what I dream?”
How do we know?
What sinks like an assassin’s bullet
to the bottom of the subconscious
therapy sofa with swift haste?

Juvenescence in juvenilia,
youthful teardrop mountain.
Feel our precipice on top
of someone else’s world.

Cognitive ego death dripping wet
with blissful discovery creatures.

I am…to be.
You are…to exist.
We are former strangers.
We are each other.
We renounce real time life.

Deluded visions higher than
the sky's natural canvas
painting extraordinary crimes.

You deem my command of language
playful and hesitant to be named.
Oh, but we are only miniscule
glimpses in lapses of denial,
societal toxin sentences,
burrowing their infectious ways
en masse, the darkness,
the peaceful darkness.

Artisanal verses in viper's dialect.
Your rendition of my
isolation song prevails in
the clusterfuck of social intimacy.

Wormwood oak mot, catching
under the tangle of the snare,
but no restraint between
our magnetic answer bodies,
burning questions with an inferno
of penned troubled chaos,
overwhelming, deafening mongers of quietude.

Breaking tension that belongs
not to us, the gemologists of
the metaphysical mavens of misery.

She is not the end; only
a parchment to the beginning.

Occupied Wall Street to
incinerate two-dimensional
green, deceased men.

Misery loves me for me,
but I refused to shake its
sonic boom hand and settle.

Fuck these blackened knuckles
of ink symbolism, the
wrong of passage meeting
with a deity's messenger,
crowning last rites.

Bleating skeletons emitting hollow sounds.
We would intervene with your
extremist warzone conflicts,
but we pacify whimsy miracles.

Though I am but an
emotionally inept wolf in the
dying dreams of the fray,
I burst forth with optimistic numbness.

Explosive orgies with nihilism's followers,
inhabiting our skin with
apocalyptic flesh engravings.

Once captivated by our
solidified unity, now hypnotized
by creation reverberating off
of the terrain of indifference.

Organic avarice into mechanical stoicism,
the future of carnal economics.

Still, she emerges a champion
from the patriarchal rubble.
Globes granting us birth,
guests in the tear ducts of the Sacred Keepers.

I make myself into a god
from a condemned portal,
but skepticism has turned me to marble.

You break me free with
a stone in love kiss and
I transition to purity in your
strengthened hands that have
wept for modern ancestry,
history's roots coming to
life's fruition in the inhaling daylight.

Radiant *Reina*, she aspires to be
with each levitating step.

Would I pass away for you?
Would I be a glutton for gullibility?
Would I starve for you?
Would I engage in limerent lust?
Would I sing for you?
Would I give my paranoid solitude away?
Would I revisit self-doubt for you?
Would I trade one vice of toxicity for another?

We are renewed, gaining warmth
from throwing our previous skin
into a ceremonial pyre.
Phantasmal swaying of the ghost dance.

III

This ghost dance kiss
viddies pristine cinema shows
about women infatuated with the dead.

The pungency, intoxicating
from the breath of lips divine,
necropolis rising between
her minds in unison with
jungle fungi in essence.

An orison lying within a kiss
emptying into whiteout wind.

Bred in captivity, but reared
in the throes of freedom thinguses.

Faith of despair, take us
into goldmine sodium water.
The sky has divorced from
aerial poesy on terrestrial
sentience of Earth.

Turn your breath into Earth,
into eighth Thursday's wine,
into a predatory spiral ending not in turmoil.

Prosaic omens dripping
down our Western Wall of sleep,
their failed orisons unanswered.

In frost and snow,
lingering, spellbound by chaotic cadavers.
Madness and sloth, licking
the corpse partner of its stillness.

Immobile meatspace rising
to the top of where we once stood,
jagged mountainside blues,
puncturing a wounded sky
with a needle zenith to
enlarge and enrapture our safe space.

Addictive bodies writhing in
the poison of ecstasy,
the venom of euphoria.

Your little death, *mi Reina*,
all I require for survival.
Our climactic nothingness,
deliberate vocal enjambment.

Pining away, the blackest pines
of yearning where we fell,
but lighter and softer than
a poem leaf meeting its
terrestrial destiny though
flesh and discontentment.

I spread my elation like
the divine firestorm of Dante,
like Lyn Lifshin spreading
her marveled seed of words
to every literary ear until
her posthumous Cliffside collapses
into a crestfallen hill of tranquility.

And when we thawed from
the tundras of denial within,
we became psychotic opinions,
confined to the American Zoo,
a patriotic cage we must transcend,
for such patriotism is misplaced.

Take the plunge straight
into my arms, Nature Girl of the
Liminal Age, yet let me bend
the law to your will

Limit my frozen answers eight.
Shut my doggerel mouth.
Shut down my dogmatic finger of time.
Let loose the cannons,
firing felines of warning
who know not of their
collective jovial fate.

Nine fold,
gates of old,
reaching for a stranded starliner.
Who screams at galaxies
without a single universal reply?

Nudity before my muse,
the shameful red of judgment.

Do ye dare look upon
the fortune of age?
Do ye dare see my
saltwater scars that bare
your name in full snarl?

A dirge for our mutual cocoon
and out we remerge with
but a demigoddess's urgency.

Never reborn,
only resumed,
for evolution's touch is
the majik of your kiss,
the lips that escape breathless moans,
beating devil heads and dulling horns,
playing discus with malevolent halos
and shotput with tumorous boulders.

We are not one,
but individualistic adhesive
who intertwine indefinitely.

I remember nothing of
smiling geology and evasive pyramids,
cursing decadence and welcoming ideologues.

Don't think twice,
it was never copacetic.

Don't cross the Sun
with an angelic wrist dial,
for when Ezekiel's hourly
acidic extraterrestrial hits,
becomes our transitional movement portal.

O' how we have entered
Dia de los Muertos in the
negative flesh, snaken year.

I met you on ancient burial grounds
on the other side of your
two-dimensional etching nativities.

Your entirety was bathed
in the birth of blood.
Sacrifice made its vibrancy
known within you, dearest
cyclical tribute woman.

Above the air where
mountain peaks pierce
the souls of clouds,
La Reina Quetzalcoatl,
Aerial Mother to you all
in half a prophet's time.

Mere physicality to the laughing eyes
which predict every reclamation.

We are all centuries in
fractured fairy stories.

Shrewd and cunning, we
exercise our right to
universal unity, bedroom momentum,
anointing each other as
autonomous beings in a non-autonomous year.

Nightwing neglect and
wolfbane whisper,
fascination makes me a part of you.

This stagnant vessel leaves no port,
the situation ship of dimmest glows.

Snakes of Jerusalem,
weeping at the Western
Separation Wall with
unanswered orisons that
we may find one another once more.

You dissipate when my eyes
look upon pre-dystopian reality.
You rematerialize when your hands
'gainst my skin activate hypnagogia.
You become a burden I yearn for
when morphing into dreamscape
from which there is no escape.

Heavenly hyperdemisexual in
a polyamorous utopia of still life,
I long for this repetitive split
soul death of ecstasy's revelations.

We have become lemniscate lovers,
ouroboros egos incinerating themselves.

Homage to every tarot fool:
his intelligence surpasses that of kings.

Pearls of passionate fashion
'round the neck of a trident-wielding
Triton laying waste, wielding to
abusers of aquatic society.

Adonis body re-sculpted to
positivity's battleground.
Toxic optimism seeping from
a masked wound held for
thirty years' time, yet escapades
found warm womb rooms,
engulfed in penalty all tombs.

Place me in my incidental palms,
and light the pyres of cremation.
Spread my ashen loveline
to the shades of evergreen,
where Love itself finds
Her truest moniker…

Pink carnations, reincarnations,
the ghost of dusk flies
to the edge of twilight.

Zah, your musical grant
has written you eighty-eight
times over, a creator's
coming together in unifying stars.

Art Herself defines you not
but the passion play that
laughs in between the lines.

Your slow dance monologues,
your sighing melodies.

We should all be so lucky,
the dragons chasing us
for euphoric reiteration,
the highs of perpetuity.

And I, your amorous documenter
of verse whose ink belongs
not to me, but the snowstorm
pages of your dulcet vocalization,
the versatility of instrumentation,
the death faces of canvas life,
the nocturnal meetings of miners.

I tell you I'm dead and gone,
and celebratory fury lights
the starry stairway in your
invigorated mind halls.

Who do you walk for in
the silver hour of empty jubilee?
Who do you cry for in
the vain spirit of disastrous night?
Who do you come for in
the dreamer's cinematic monologue?

My silent film tongue
shrieks your name as my
Pompeii lava river bursts in
between colosseum columns,
gripping palmistry readings
so that our slumber lasts for
but a perilous fortnight.
I was here nary a minute ago.

The dregs fucked us in
their world of lizard royalty.

Ragged, yet regal as
a commoner thief of wealth,
we drift through the
restlessness of walking corpse
prosperity and into a
newfangled land of fictitious genesis.

Qualitative in the superficial.
Jaundice golden like the
hair of those I notice not
as I wade thru' the poppy field
to entangle myself in your raven strands.

We are cinnamon that
honey can only dream of,
but the drone's death overflows
with nectar from forehead
to nipple's first glance,
a decade's honor among
images of a bedside absence,
restored to the fullness of time.

Bland voice in a seasoned
world of crossover color,
the material of our true nature
is the lie of digital sentences
they speak for us as we
drown in the data of hostility.

Terabytes of fascism,
Terra no more, lost to a
domineering web of falsifiers.
Totality eclipses the
early afternoon of darkness,
have we any hope for the
individualized reckoning,
the becoming of independency?

We are free thinkers, paying
the price for the oligarchy
of chauvinistic theocracy,
the mania of misogynistic
mercy killings of the divine feminine soul,
so sayeth the Supreme Cult.

Why is eternal division
your love letter to the
monotheistic man child?
Why is the removal of
woman power your salivating glee?
Why are the Firsts
still residing on the
bare bones that ivory spat upon?
Why does segregation race
against ancestral timelines?

Amidst the crossroads of
tonality's chaos, there She stands,
one-eighth of my Venus-
laden soul bond soldier.

Amidst the decrepit mountain
of scattered soothsayer knowledge,
always on your side for
the boundless evers that
spell the name you told me
to give you: Moonrider Elder.

Lunar overseer, where the
heart beats with rapidity
upon your curvature's arrival.

Like an atomic bomb on impact,
we clash with playful gasps
of heated elation, oh how
my imploding world believes
in a greater faith than
Abrahamic god texts, holy
outdated futurism acts.

We walk amongst the
perfectly symmetrical pebbles
that kiss our laughs of hydration,
that seal our armored fate.

What is vulnerability without chance?
An open, festering gash
that supersedes all logic.

The redemption claim
is victimized fame,
and yet my balance exterminates the ceiling.

If your cricket mind
is vacant, may I occupy
the sugarwall corner of
your honey-dipped composure?

Empty stars and empty spaces,
the clemency of highest excellence.
Your morning scent trails
towards me as a lingering
parasitic host of a friend,
the banging of melodic doom.

The wizard of the enchanted sea
fills our minds with meadowland.

Stagnation, cutting dusk
with the knife that seeks
out angels on cocaine mountains.
Philosophize o'er me,
my smoking gun bite-marks.

Cross-eyed answers ask
themselves why they
lack substance of vision.

Some dream heroine
becoming her own story
in Avalonian mists that
no man can penetrate.

Dream believer, waking up
to slumberous awakenings,
to accidental purposes,
to the death of life,
to the most truthful lie.

Her womb is a window for
her own mortality's splendor,
a door for reincarnated silhouettes.

Let me be her riddle unanswered,
her unfinished Xanadu reverie.

Hand turns to paw by the
silvery glisten of moonstruck water
we drank from the
blackest blood reflections,
feeling murderous sacrifice
transform into animalistic duality.

Dichotomous conflict of
spiritus and thingus,
the physique of mentality.

What would we be without
breath stealers suppressing
their innermost delirium secrets?

Dreadnoughts composing
epic essays that gush ink,
reek of relevant tangents,
Tulgey Wood signs of ambiguity.

Castaway meltdown of
islandic abandonment, for
only the loneliest of elements
can reunite the lingering star,
ampleness of ashen galaxies.

Somewhere the King of Night
cries for a broken commoner's crown.

Dilute my pleasure.
Become my pain.
Darkened cloud of heathenist nightshade.

IV

This heathenist nightshade kiss
is but a forlorn thought,
ephemeral and fleeting,
illusion of vibrating lips,
the sensation of a killer's touch.

Crawling skin on the
boneyard spine of misunderstood monsters.

Death pardons those which
have regressed into flickering beacons.

I forgo the melancholic sea
and drift towards your
nether tongue that feigns speech.
Demonic perspective on the
turning of blissful tides.

Hourglass angels letting
time slip through their sand grain fingers.
Bleeding resistance through
their shameful eyes
through every ghastly ghoul,
every bastardized creature,
every misrepresented cryptid,
every abandoned specter,
every psychic vampire,
every neglected Promethean man,
every sleep-deprived mummy,
every cursed blessing of the werewolf.

I see only you, lover beyond
every *Madre Tierra* tree,
modest savior, humble heroine
amidst a field of honey
where our first mutual caress
made its own chapter of history.

Planting my breath
on your exposed navel,
your desert ground midriff.

My forehead between the
hillsides of your breasts
where serenity knows no end
in this cruel, daunting,
nonlinear simulation we call life.

Falling in love with the
possession of our dialogue,
how our words trek to distant
destinations with no formal conclusion
in bittersweet sight.

Fate, dearest amorous fate,
is a midday trance that
lasts for every lifetime,
but why the chandelier moves
to the center astral ceiling,
only the projectionist knows.

Sudden insolence, speaking
of woes untold thru' the
threadbare politics of emotion.

We emerge from howling snows
and into the arid ruins
where your ancestry's
noble mark laid to rest
their final skeletal song,
their final A to Q.

Birds of elder flight,
taking to seaworthy heights
for neutral buoyancy shelters,
squawking theories with
castle paupers and hordes
of Skaven princes in crying rooms.

Vermillion vermin in the skirmish,
tsunami awash with vanishing
isles, tropical hell, sinking with change.

Blue bloodstones being paid for their crimes,
climaxing when violence strikes,
but never toward our faint barrier,
now a tarnished speck of metal liquid.

I melt in your arms of
speculative fiction,
a fraction of escapist pages.

I beg for fantastical sanctuary,
an ask from the bowels of Tartarus
meadows on a glimmering leash.
It's all relative, *querida*.

To don chain and collar
Is to walk with the horizontal
noose of forgiveness.
To blow the trumpets of sordid
zero atmosphere is to
whitewash history unmade,
the screeching truths splashed
with ivory superiority machines.

We have surpassed and
transcended the dancing
shepherds of fascist hands,
the octopi of treasonous ink.

We call the faithful to
their vocalized composition,
oscillating between left riots
and right monstrosity, the
abominable stoic median,
laughing and shrugging
and bleating and squealing
and moaning and succumbing.

Sing of the dead tonight.
Cancion de la Muertas.
Why only a day for the
transparent celestials?
Why only a stanza
for the Transcendentalists,
warlocks killing written sound?

All hail literacy's uprising,
sans a dictator's demographic.

You are my fairy anthology,
your jacket collecting dust
from the raw introspective
of the demise of borrowed time.

You loaned me your soul
improvisations without notice
of eternal third eye deafness,
without blinding Helios lights
to sun-kissed clairaudients.

I will crumble my deconstructed
statue for the good of humanity.

To lay in freshest wheat fields,
forces reckoning without our say so.

Death weeps…
…with elation.
The coolness of scythe slides
across my skin of consent,
to slash and pass away
another downtrodden day.

Mirrors and smoke,
smoke and mirrors,
I abandoned self-love for moonshot fears.

Smoke and mirrors,
mirrors and smoke,
you left me behind for the cross-bearing folk.

Spellcasting outcasts
in some Stonehenge facility,
dying faces immortalized
in a wall of great mortality,
atom heart mothers belting
out pastoral choir arrangements.

Shrewd downpour of rain
was never an option, for
we began as a dream of a
human in cosmic unity with themselves.

And after orgasmic tremors,
exit in the orb emerald of memory,
a memory of the human in
tamed wilderness, yet unleashed
in the carnal world of red rage.

Nestled in the talons of the
Lord Falcon, Skywing Bard,
guardian of another yesterday.

We are transported to
ethereal tiger green world.

I cannot take this tranquil treachery.
I cannot take its striped
glacier without the
tragedy of strategy,
the ruthless salt that
attacked the freshness of wounds.

Walking a fine line
between comet tapestries
and the vultures
who scavenged what's left
of our lover's naïveté,
the luxury of being lost,
now an afterthought,
dedicated to the fell beast
of transparent saturation.

Beating the dolls' heads,
plastic souls emitting
white noise in steampunk
revelations and clockwork
epiphanies striking eight,
the cuckoo introducing itself
like a viper's fang on
a sullen creature's red right shoulder.

In the mist of December,
I always see you
writing my name in hearts,
the juvenile fantasy
taking control of
jaded *amarillo* and
tantric silver overlapping
one another in frenzied
waves of miraculous magnetism.

The heat of a moment
that wakes from every
nocturnal vision, ending
in sweet emission of biology's nectar,
made from the chemical of intimacy.
Now foreign to me
in your glorified absence,
I cannot accept oxygen
without your distant hand's approval.

I thought we had seen
the bard's accentuated intellect,
now shrouded in stealthy
rainbows of children's
delights, delectable succubae fungus.

Nijinsky dreams in
Judas waking nightmare,
for I am walking on desert air,
where the reddened dust
is a storm of words
that we cannot brave, the
violence with pink mist silence.

O'the maroon silo hears
what the lighthouse rumors
tell the audience of grains.

Dragon shadow donning
fur-scaled coat of fog.

Lapping up the lake water
of frozen summer sun drops.
I cannot believe my liquid windows.

O' Mesopotamian star shriek!
Emerge, she does,
Enheduanna, the first
signature of verse, the first
nomenclature solidifying
Inanna tribute stanzas.

Priestess of golden temples so fair,
guiding my orb-laden lover
to the Saffron Tower
where we once laid.

Sifting through the ashes
of bipartisan futility,
we stand against their
tides of division, their
riotous vanity for the
want of shameless desire.

We stroll away from
their tantrum stances about face,
bleeding wealth like oil.

This land was not a clue,
a spiritual conscience
to rid the colonized swine bellies.

We laugh at the ivory blaze
and sprint towards a blank utopia.

We speak with our feet,
communicate with our chests,
scream with our hands…

And still, the *chisme* is deafening.
And still, the gossiping crook
of the winds in Albion time
slinks through the vastness of trenches.

Mud and a stock of wood,
musical orgy in the sensationalized
fields, she knew me when
I was that tempest thief.
She was the gale girl who
intersected with my force of nature.

Though we were meant to
dance in the haze o suave hullaballoo,
the joys of frustration kept
us afloat, our weeping wallets
committing the act of zeros.

I remember not who I was when
holding your repaired spirit against mine,
but the sparklecat bodies
we were beneath the ancient tree ring
exterior, caking us with
soil unreformed, yet peace
in spades ravages war-torn
hellbound wings, to any
other culture's creation realm.

We writhe about in the
portal's realm like poets
craving a written fix.

Supersonic music, captivating
all of us in contortionist gasps.

Cellophane amoebas beating
heartbeat style in a wild
room in the wing of a wish.

I wish for you…
I wish for us…
I wish for me…
I wish for all…
One, on the permanent
side of the mirror.

Ablaze with flaming blades,
awash with flushed emotion.

All curiosity becomes a
tale of barebacked glory,
a fateful night, an orgasm's story.

Why does the tantric pouring
of manna end as
quickly as a blinking bolt?
Why must the freezing over
of a theoretical hell punish
Earthlings who have made
this geography a part of themselves.

Solemn stone, sullen sky,
a metropolis of suburban country.
Suburbia's city among a
mandala psychedelic glove,
removing itself from the
staring aural note, hitting
every key and chord in
a liminal pleasure, ah, me…

A freshened thrill approaching
us on the stillness of
a bent horizon painting,
hearing colors for the first time.

Radio waves looping dialogue,
for a diagonal mind.

Here we sit,
here we drift
to the jungle mountain,
conquering our fearful
reservations of a burning future.

The temptations of poetry
mean little to our escapist
mindheart worlds…

Fault me not for exorcising
what demons of hatred
I harbored for the grand exit.

Our nation of life's next
earful of netherworld rumors…
Still, the reiki chakras rise.

And back to the broken
mirror shard you left me,
only to watch you leave
shattered ambition behind in
the lair of language.

Dropped anchor in the only
sea of tranquility awakenings,
awakened tranquility in
the psychosis of a mind star.

Head cinema playing repeated
films of our abysmal courtship
and ecstatic uprising.

How have we survived tribulations
in the provocative estuary?
How have we gathered a
pointed star for throwing
into the love-made aerial window?

Echoes of reflections gone,
yet not mentioned for
fruitful, avoidant mechanisms.

We feel lightheaded in the
afterglow of last night's
tomorrow party, the Mala,
the Western Rapture,
the visible glimpse of Mama Aya.

Mama Aya, are you proud?
Do you approve of us shifting
galaxies in the wake of
a writer's sudden momentum?
Do you yourself slumber
in the diurnal hours as
Peruvian guests await your
universal proclamations?

Show us endless genealogy carvings
and an end to the wisest
of able-headed bloodlines.

Are the orally-birthed snakes
worth the tangential discovery?

Ride my battle-hardened words with
simultaneous gasps of euphoric death.

V

This euphoric death kiss
is a rainfall of horses,
a star exiting the fist
when one ankh enters
the other in relevant fury.

Samhain in the Underworld,
blackened pumpkin king in
the good bones of my home.

Heartbreakers finish strong
in the shielding walkthrough.

Oh, my word!
The cinders have amassed
into a winter's day,
such is enriched lifeblood.

Empaths on a separate path,
the aroma of sound.
From each of the amplified
Hundred Year War wounds,
their energy drained of
all floodgate past lives.

We deserve not this
incarnation of trust,
never constructed for the
pillar of unconditional love.

We deserve not unconditional love,
for among humans, it is
a deity invisible in the
matter of elegant ether.

I met you in the wholehearted
grain of incomprehensible *amor*.

Your turn the vagrant's page
to reveal a dawn-touched
amulet of topaz, call
my month by pet name,
mythical outwaters in
nonlinear years, for
you hold the only treasure
that matters in the
bittersweet, subjective end.

Why wield words in
this rustic life?

Why not give up *amor*
when She turned her back
on us for millennia untold?

Who has transcribed your
tear stains onto feathered
Cirrus impressions?

The vibrations have been
with us all along, dearest.

Damn the lizards of limerence
to the volcanic median
of the three-sided coin,
this spherical Earth.

We have received the wondrous vision tale!
Gross judgments snapping
to an unkempt conclusion.

We have redefined the
platinum in between
the knuckles of
parchment's blood in sensuous fruit.

Under the hill and through the bones,
ruminating until the swine
sends hope to the dogs.

They speak in blood,
yet howl in empty vanity.

Your papyrus syllables are no more.
They are only vows not
taken by 21st century
marriages who turn the other way.

This night cascades over us
like a drape of misty fabric,
cloaking us from what
has been and what was once hid.

Valley storm and primordial vigor,
out fly the arthropods of fire
from rejected sparks.

We glanced at one another,
and away'd into the
mundane condition of
humanity's forebears.

I know your face from
some violet fever dream
where we frenzied our way
towards each other's inner
circle of idiosyncratic truth.

You took my hand and deemed
me a precious spirit of wandering.
I took your hand and deemed
you savior sans complex.

Slithering failsafe watch wolf,
lumbering boulder doves,
insomnia's second cousin's
head twice removed.

You know my face from
nightmare hero *chisme*,
eight glorious metals
that flow through rocky
veins an into the
solar flesh of lunar carnivores.

I see only a split nocturnal mind.
Silence is met with
the hounds of anguish,
for we all decay a little
more each day on the planet
begging us to return what
we have stolen over time's dark hand,
the green of *La Reina's* body.

And with catastrophic reverence,
our meatspaces are yours
to feast upon with the
tangled mouths of vines.

Failing uncertainty in
reemergence of our melodic
downfall of a species of futility.

Our hands struggle to each
one another in apocalyptic
hours of mute desperation.

But, we succeed and fly
like fools from their sinking
ship downward to a watery cemetery.

We have always bonded
over trauma's seduction
and have connected
over tragedy's temptations,
but no more, for the
ceremonial skins have been shed,
making way for glistening,
reincarnated question marks,
willing to struggle with
incantations that lose
doubt within themselves.

The fragile mystic hath been hexed!
A curse called 'stagnation of life',
a blessing of death's
boundless gardens of infinity.

Still, we fled to a more
isolated corner of a land
heard only in sundial realms.

I kiss your third eye's monocle
and we are transported to
visual stimulation forest,
where the flora engages
in unmuddied dialogue
and the fauna encourage
the art of spiritual electricity.

They say the word is
'Orenda', but what will
cause massive change
amongst the Original Autochthonous?

What will blossom to be,
those whose minds
now belonged to bipedal vultures,
picking clean the source
of fecund morbidity?

A glass magenta midnight
to Bharat, the true soul name
of a bountiful lover's location.
Hindustan, the Middle Forceful Hand
called it for their own secular convenience.
India, Cross-Eyed Westerners
claimed the nomenclature like a rescue canine.

"Now, where were we?
Ah, yes!" pondered the holy
detectives as we trudge
through our lapsed odyssey.

Breaking poems in threes
until the gryphon's wings
match out combined energy.

We are suburban savages
in a metropolis that
regurgitates us among the gridlock
like the ocean's surf rejecting
its rugged riders of sighs.

We have reclaimed ourselves
in the fashion of Circles Nine.
I endured Hell's assortment
of pleasures to find you.
I romped through Elysian illusions
to tell you to be your own human.
I could never cast you out
like a shadow of a mental exorcism.

Within my burdened palm's
affluent lines are perpendicular orphans
where meditation and prayer
cohabitate with the
same gestures as yours.

Ave Satanas,
She is a woman of the
most noble breed, welcoming
you with open auras
and universally conceptual arms.

From chakras to empty taps,
we lunge towards a truth
proving more than an accentuated
humanity and its frail prosperity.

More toasts to the fawn of fauna,
the grassy floor of flora,
that ignites green, grinning,
grim remembrances that only
a mother's radio face could love.

Thirteen rocks and filthy mondegreens,
we heard what we thought
was the dynamo message that
could bear to listen to one more generation.

The weight of the season,
the height of the treason,
the trees in the median
of the loner ice flow.

When will our hearts melt
for one another again?

Indigo laughing into a dance
that the whiteness of oblivion
orchids adorning your physique.
The complexion of centuries
unraveled, your inferno head
combusting with the
spontaneity of former romantic,
useless husks for
biological decoration…

You traitor of conversation pieces,
you lamenting glass figurine.

We must away into
the abolished nightscape,
the tarnished day score.

And we drift 'cross
the tidy penny room,
dreadful as the purple door.

Behind it, hemorrhaging our
collective name in jade.
Perseverance is how we
have made a home in the
still death portrait of art.

Be not the widow head,
with a Picasso body withering
upon my temporary absence.

Grief is lingering death
like an aroma that love
dares to forget in its entirety.

Beggars choose not,
pornographers viddy not,
ambiverts flow always.

Greet my lips and you're lovely.
You better look now, for the
Giant Mother Sea swallows
and envelops us whole for
the sake of a convoluted evolution.

Pioneering no frontier but
the reckoning of our own.

We oversee the acoustics
of this safe space which
belongs to the center of
derangement, oh, my bloody luck.

I would take thee in my arm,
only to feel you slipping through
my fingers, pale and unencumbered.

I have drank my fill from
youth's bleak fountain,
only to discover the childlike
wonder I once was when
the heaving monolith collapsed.

Wide-eyed soulless sockets
you evolve from cave shades,
into the dust of singularity
collected by the jackals
of revolutionary solidarity.

What a blinding thrill you are.
What a winter's breathy chill
it is to be with your hillside manner.

What an honor it is to
climb your egotism spires,
to aspire to new levels of faith,
to give in to the sweet release of fate.

Fall.
Fail.
Field.
Fear.

I have fallen for your,
but why this Sister Moon heart?
Why choose me to fall,
a bumbling, stumbling
landfill of parasitic doubts?

Venus whispers turn to
succubae screams, liberation
for the allies, *Santa Muerte's*
bruja dancing a jig in
half-curved moonlight,
a fraction of oneself to
free love in ghost plumes.

Oh, you incontrovertible arrow,
hitting the void where
my heart should reside,
yet dormancy *in absentia* is a square flame.

Is the pain a poem?
Divine intervention of nothingness,
electrical majesty in
deafening, orgasmic delight.

Pretty little flower in betwixt your jet hair,
a sapphire twinkle as you convulse.

The sacred walls closing in,
providing euphoric suffocation.

Sweet euphoria,
how we transcend our
tangible vessels and play
amongst the astral forests of the Sun.
Your afterglow river face
reflects off mine in
liquid emulation, solid perfection.

Thoth writes us out in
bitter papyrus, sun-dialed and paper-thick.

Enkidu, entranced by your
timeless beauty, walks
you to the epicenter of
primeval art in civilized livelihood.

You were assembled
of pure, unadulterated light,
and I from the breath
a restless seer devoted
to the will of Gaia's eye.

She licks controversy's
anal cavity and leads
smoke-made fleets
of phantom liners to
the acidic, digestive darkness.
Lack of pride is hell to digest.

Swallowing gaseous crystals,
we hover o'er the generous
ice volcanoes, sparing us
from a blazing rush of coldth.

I am rabid for you, *mi querida*,
and I cannot cease the foaming
blasts of ambiguity.

I am hungry for you, *mi querida*,
and I cannot sate the creature within me.

My lions are magnets towards you, *mi querida*,
but their stride breaks when your awakened
lion flesh enters every room.
And how you enter, dearest,
meandering orb light
from the ethereal dominions where
we first abandoned linear logic
for abstract passion.

How have we held one another
for this long?
How have we not yet dissolved?

Silvery starlight,
pipe dream moonbeams,
swearing us in by honor alone,
descending from courts on high,
Olympian chaos,
Q's bloodwing sacrifice,
a promise birthed from *sangre*,
a promise broken by stone,
and for *what*, my dearest?

Time's trickster side was never on ours.
We have lived curiosity's fantasy
and it has killed our feline lives
nine times over in rapid succession.

The blink of softened globe bones
hides behind the almighty
royalty dollar structure,
winking at the top of pyramids
built by geological giants.

How can mere mortals
bride immortal gaps when
the winded blow is our game?

And as the Green Fairy
glides in on an absinthe vapor,
one hand becomes intertwined
with hers when the vision
is peripheral and petrified.

How will sight reunite us?
Intervals…passing…why?

We are not futurists, but
clingers to the ashes of the past,
unresolved puzzles separated.

Hesitation of inhibitions,
lowering upon first glimpse.
We are not us in the
morning coo of grief-stricken doves.

Eloquence becomes you,
your tongue of momentary speech,
your tongue tangoing 'gainst mine
in a psychotropic fury.

Thrust us not in the limelight,
but into the dead of day,
scatterbrained discourses
seeking solace in our
eight limbs in an arachnophilic mania.

Sky fire above electric ice.
We are still falling for one another.

Lose you not to the
despondent gods, destroyers
of the forgiving harvest.

You knew no regret until
harmony's elevated brow
leads us to a newfangled sense of semi-belonging.
I'm crouching,
I'm prostrating,
I'm seeing jasmine.

Your lilac garden corner,
resting comfortably in
the solar confines of
your childish brain.

My two cells greet your
million as desperate stragglers
from another dimensional room
burst forth with clawed
exhibition shows sans a screech.

Oh, take me for the final
go round, the Devil's carousel,
the whittling away of onset
paranoia, gateways of this life.

Nary a blemish on the
coldest of shoulder blades, the
mythology of your murmur.

We care not, for we tumble
heads over feet, the defense
of substantial elegance,
dripping from my feet to yours.

This provincial chapter
is not real, but the touch
of zest and zeal, faint-hearted
lover of every age.

You are my face,
declaring our eternal vow
that our bodies made
through the physicality of words.

Expression is lack of
vocalization through the
oral orifice of oracles.

It is the aural reply,
the visual stance that
obliterates the perpetuation
of universal oppression.

Your heart warmth,
beating my barrier's collection
of assorted shields to death
until we celebrate vulnerability's vastness.

Sink to me, your dark-lipped song.
Home and away again, amorous flashes.

As our demise diminishes, so do I,
in the boundless haven of your kiss.

May 30-September 30, 2024

The Basorexia Song

And when you gaze into
my plucked soul with your
Amityville eyes,
I celebrate denial's entrance,
luck being the lady you are,
the lightning lover who electrifies.

I'm nobody's fool but yours,
nobody's serpent staff of the Nile.
I'm nobody's sheep but yours,
nobody's instrument of death on the Emerald Mile.

The Sun singing fog presides
o'er our model village towards the skies.
Can you resolve blessed damnation?
Symbol of our name, a modern antique.
Portmanteau of our gasping goddesses,
a future looking desperately bleak.
Is it love that befuddles me,
or the planetary sigil that speaks?

Rising Moon of the Leviathan's hiss,
locked away in the promise of a dusky kiss.

Eight basorexian years since the fleeting
moment that drew us together,
a self-portrait to which we toast.
Watching you levitate like
the daughter of mystic revolution,
the maiden's willowing ghost.

Euphoric life shadows
dissipate with the will of curtain clouds.
Wailing spiritus of our climactic wake,
deepened slumber before the Reaper's shroud.

My prison cell was the
sliver of doubt that festered,
the starspot wound of galactic infection.
Long-winded farcical speeches
made in the neon of a shallow breeze.
May I be deemed your object of affection?
I require no external protection
but the inferno's roaring connection.

Baby, there must be something amiss.
First time thrill of an amnesiac's kiss.

If only we had encountered
one another in a moving photograph,
celluloid phantom preservation.
Sensationalized specters,
romanticized ravers,
all bopping to silent, musical formation.

Find me at the crossing
of the Juarez bullet casings and mercy.
Found you at the *ciudad* café,
composing passion flame verses.

We clean ourselves of
rumored remarks in the
fashion of stoic statues,
in denial of their own motion.
Throwing rose petals to the wind,
patchouli to the arrowed backs.
The last kill is our first entry
as we fall under the spell of the *bruja's* floral potion.

Rescue me from the pewter abyss,
and hold me close to the warmth of your kiss.

Can I be your overcomer
of hypocritical, monotheistic
pain in the hesitant heart?
This is no game of exaggeration.
This is not a limerence illusion,
for we were meant to be from the commentary's start.

Break your seasonal footing
for the sake of shadowed tradition.
Radical extremist creation myths
for a Progresso pyramid expedition.

Es tu cabeza la estrella?
Cold progress over the Moon,
the suburban blasphemy of comfort.
Es tu cancion la poema?
Paz stanzas, gleaming like
fresh ink drafts penetrating the soft hurt.

Cracking a half-smile as we reminisce,
the flashback of the first fiery kiss.
Forever seeking asylum of bargained bliss,
the climactic, limitless consistency of your kiss.

September 28, 2024

Basorexia: The overwhelming desire to kiss

This has been a nonlinear epic straight from the hyperphantasia-laden lunacy of Z.M. Wise.

About the Author

Z.M. Wise is a proud Illinois native from the Northwest Suburbs of Chicago, poet, vocalist/lyricist/songwriter, essayist, occasional playwright, seldom screenwriter, editor, and arts activist, writing since his first steps as a child. He was selected to be a performer in the Word Around Town Tour in 2013, a Houston citywide tour. He is co-owner and co-editor of Transcendent Zero Press, an independent publishing house for poetry that once produced an international quarterly journal known as *Harbinger Asylum*. The journal was nominated Best Poetry Journal in 2013 at the National Poetry Awards. He is the author of several full-length books and chapbooks of poetry, as well as a play. In mid-2023, Wise collaborated with well-known musician A.J. Kaufmann to release Ch'ulel, a collaborative/split album where they both played instruments, sang, and composed lyrics. Other than the aforementioned books and album,his poems, lyrics, short fiction, essays, and book reviews have been published in various journals, magazines, and anthologies. The motto that keeps him going: POETRY LIVES AND LONG LIVE THE ARTS! Wise will make sure to spread that message and the love of the arts, making sure it remains vibrant for the rest of his days and beyond. Besides poetry and other forms of writing, his other passions/interests include playing a few instruments, creative & professional voice acting, creating visual art, cooking/baking, fitness, and reading.

www.ingramcontent.com/pod-product-compliance
Lightning Source LLC
LaVergne TN
LVHW050603160826
845677LV00011B/2437

* 9 7 8 2 4 8 7 0 1 7 0 7 8 *